LIFE
PROBLEMS?
STUDY
PROBLEMS?
NO
PROBLEM!

LIFE
PROBLEMS?
STUDY
PROBLEMS?
NO
PROBLEM!

PATRICK NG

PARTRIDGE
A Penguin Random House Company

To order additional copies of this book, contact
Toll Free 800 101 2657 (Singapore)
Toll Free 1 800 81 7340 (Malaysia)
orders.singapore@partridgepublishing.com

www.partridgepublishing.com/singapore

CONTENTS

To my family, who gave me helpful comments, and especially my son, who financially helped me in the process, and my daughter, who laboriously read through my book. I am also thankful to Mr. Siva, who helped me type out my book. I also thank the Partridge Singapore staff who guided me through the whole process, especially Mr. Jo Blanco, who also gave me words of encouragement.

WHEN I WAS YOUNG

In 1958, when I was in standard five, my father died of gangrene. I knew that our family was going to face financial problems, as my father was the sole breadwinner. I was very afraid, fearful that I would have no food to eat and have to sleep on the street. My mother cried every day, and I would sit beside her and console her, but she cried even more. I realized she was thinking that she would be forced to give us away to others. I was afraid to have to leave her for another family, so I began to pray to God to help us. I prayed and prayed and prayed for many days. I asked Mother Mary to implore her Son Jesus to help us. I did not ask

Jesus directly to help us, for I thought that it would be proper to ask His mother first.

Did Jesus answer me? Yes, He did, in a very special way. You see, my father worked for a private company, yet he was not entitled to any pension. But a miracle happened. One day, a European man and a Chinese man walked into our house and talked to my mother. The European spoke in English while the Chinese man translated his words into Chinese for my mother. He asked whether my mother intended to marry again, to which my mother replied that she would not. Then the Chinese man asked my mother whether our house was already paid for. My mother answered sadly that the house was still under installments and she would have to pay RM 90 per month. The two gentlemen left after talking with my mother.

Several days later, a piece of good news came. My mother was told that the company would give my mother RM 150 per month to help her. With this money, my mother was able to pay the house installments and raise us. This was a real miracle of faith in God. The financial difficulty that we faced was taken up to heaven, and that difficulty was no longer on my mother's shoulders. The yoke was lifted!

However, the RM 60 left after paying the house installments was not enough to buy good food for my two brothers, three sisters, and me. I had to bring food to school to eat during school recess. My food consisted of bread with coconut, fried with brown sugar. My classmates laughed at me, saying I was eating shit. I was embarrassed and had to take my food to the toilet to avoid them seeing me eat.

Again, I prayed to Jesus for help. I prayed each day I went to school. I even cried without anyone noticing and said to myself, "How long will I have to bear this? Jesus, help me."

Then He answered. I accidentally came across an elderly woman who knew my mother, and she was staying around my school. She said she pitied me, for I was fatherless, so she gave me fifty cents every day to eat in the school canteen. I could eat Chinese noodles and drink a glass of ice water. The noodles cost twenty cents a bowl, and the ice water was five cents a glass. After school, I would use the balance of twenty-five cents to buy tidbits and pay for my bus fare. Jesus answered me in a special way. I went on surviving like this and feeling so thankful for His help.

During my days in school when I was between the ages of eleven and twelve years old (standard five and six), I was indeed very sad because I could not read or write. My brother used to tease me by asking me to read the covers of my books. I felt very shameful. I did not know how to read. I felt it would be better if I became an ant and crawled away to hide. I prayed to Jesus to help me, but the answer did not come immediately.

Then one day when I was in standard six, my teacher asked me to memorize a phrase in the Catholicism book and to read out the phrase to her the next day in school. The phrase was "Why did God make you?" The answer was "God made me to know Him, to serve Him, and to be with Him forever in the next."

I prayed to Jesus very intensely, and at the same time, I read the phrase over and over many times. I even put the Catholicism book under my head to sleep. The next day, I was asked to repeat that memorized phrase "Why did God make you?" I answered, feeling Jesus was with me, "God made me to know Him, to serve Him, and to be with Him forever in the next."

I felt very happy, and I knew that Jesus answered me. And from then on, I was able to read, write, and memorize.

When I Reached Adulthood

In 1968 when I was nineteen and with a grade three Cambridge school certificate, I got a job as a clerk in a legal firm. I spent eight years hopping from legal firm to legal firm. After that, I wanted to do something better and have a better job, but I had no money to study. I needed time to study and to have some money to pay for my school fees.

I asked Jesus for guidance, and after much consideration, I left my job to sell beef soup noodles. This new job gave me more free time and a bit of money to survive and to pay for my school fees. I would take a book to read beside my small stall at the roadside. I was studying for the Association of Business Executives (ABE) examination. Because I did not have a form six Cambridge school certificate and I did not intend to take A levels, I took this ABE certificate instead. With the help of Jesus Christ, I passed the ABE examinations and went on to sit for the diploma.

I prayed whenever I could not understand parts of my studies. I prayed with much faith and confidence to attain success in my studies. I always prayed to Jesus before I went to bed, to the extent that I dreamed of Him putting His hand over my head. Jesus did open my mind even though I was a slow learner. I would ask Jesus to knock open my head so He could place knowledge into my brain. Then when I had received His blessings, I would go to a chapel to give thanks to the Lord.

Finally, I completed the ABE advanced diploma through self-study and with the help of Jesus.

I Argued with a Teacher

I took my ABE diploma at the Ge Te Institution, the largest college in Penang at that time. The college had more than two thousand students. When I graduated with the ABE diploma in business administration, I worked as a clerk in this college because I only had experience in this line. My aim was to be a lecturer, but I had no experience and courage yet. While working as a clerk, I prayed to Jesus to give me a chance to become a lecturer. This time, my prayer was answered in a very special way.

One day, a lecturer argued with me over why my typing was so slow. I argued with him and put forward my arguments with him in an ardent manner, and I won. The boss of the Ge Te Institution looked on and heard my reasoned answer. He then told me to take a class of six students and teach them accounting. My assignment was to maintain the number of students until the end of the one-year course. If the class dwindled, I would have to leave the job. Oh, what a task!

I thought to myself, *Jesus, how to do this?* I closed my eyes and knelt down beside my bed every night to pray, "Jesus, have mercy on me. Help me to remain in my post as a lecturer. Mother Mary, implore your Son Jesus to help me!"

Did Jesus help me? Yes! As I lectured, I felt that He was beside me, and I pictured that He put forward His hands to lift me up. He lifted up my fear and torment because my class began to increase in number, growing in size to more than twenty students. The boss of the college told me that the students liked me and said he would put me in charge of a larger class in the next intake. I was overjoyed and thanked Jesus. I said, "I thank You, Jesus. You have always been my Savior. You raise me up in stormy sea and lift me up when I am in troubles. I remain Your humble servant. Patrick Ng."

I taught in this college for five years.

THE NEXT LEVEL OF THE POWER OF CHRIST

One day as I was going to Ge Te institution to lecture, to my surprise, I saw many people gathered outside the school. I was told that the school was closed. I tried to find my boss, but he was not around. The next day, I went to school again, and I found the doors closed this time. I thought that my career would be finished. Ge Te was the largest college in Penang.

Again, I prayed to Him for help. I invoked Mother Mary to implore Jesus to find me a post as a lecturer. I prayed and prayed. Then I read in the papers that a new college was opening in Penang, Institute of Perkim Goon. I applied for a job as a lecturer in accounting, and I was given a post. My starting pay was slightly higher than my previous post at Ge Te institution.

I was extremely happy, and I thanked God for this opportune time. Teaching at Perkim Goon helped me become better in my job and made me want to teach higher-level courses. So after years of lecturing in Perkim Goon, I applied for a lecturing post at Cyma College, Penang. Here, I was to teach the final paper in accounting of the Chartered Institute of Management Accountants (CIMA) course.

I needed God's help very urgently, and I knew that, if He failed me, I would fail. I had to read a lot to gather information on this difficult accounting subject. To gather more information at this level, I had to read and understand quickly. I said to myself, "God, give me a spark of Your power and open up my mind to understanding."

I asked and begged him to open up my mind. But my mind could not go further, and I thought I had to give up at this point.

He Opened My Mind

Then a miracle happened. He did help me but in a rather indirect way. One day, I went to visit my sister, whose husband was a lawyer. My late brother-in-law told me a very effective way to study. He said our brain is like pigeonholes and studying is like filling up those holes. And on completion of filling those holes, we will understand our study. I began to ponder upon those words. But how to fill up those holes quickly? I tried and tried, but I was still so slow, and it was so difficult to fill up all those holes.

Then that inner voice spoke again, "Read the whole book through quickly."

I did accordingly, and I read through an article quickly. I found that I understood nothing when I had finished reading. I read it again, this time paying more attention and trying to pick up meaning of the sentences. By now, I had finished reading the article a second time. Then I read over the article a third time to try to understand more, and I found that I finally understood what the article was saying. I asked students to ask me questions based on the article, and when I answered them correctly, I knew I had found the solution.

STUDY IN TOTAL

I began to read my tax book using the same method. I took up an economics book, and I read over three hundred pages in one month's time. So each day, I read ten pages, and in over thirty days, I finished the book. Then I read the book a second time within the same time frame but with a keener understanding. And after the second reading, I was able to answer about 70 percent of questions asked in the book. I tried doing the same thing with other books, like accounting. I aimed to finish the whole book quickly, like reading a storybook, and I found out that, by finishing the whole book first, we get to see the whole picture. Later readings helped me fill the pigeonholes in my mind with detailed information.

Here are the steps that you have to follow:

First Reading

1. Close your eyes and relax. Call upon Jesus to help you understand quickly and easily.

2. With your eyes closed, build up an energy force in your mind by visualizing that Jesus is transmitting His light through His hand on your head.

3. Read each page using about ten minutes apiece. Then put aside the book after reading ten pages, and read other books or do something else.

4. The next day, repeat steps one through three until you finish the whole book.

For a book with three hundred pages, you would have taken thirty days to finish.

Second Reading

1. Follow the above steps—one through four—until you finish the whole book, but this time, try to absorb the meaning of each page you read.

Third Reading

1. Read aloud using the method in the second reading until you finish the whole book.

2. Don't be afraid that you would not succeed, for Jesus had said, "If you had faith as big as a mustard seed, you could say to this mulberry tree, 'Pull yourself up by the roots and plant yourself in the sea' and it would obey you" (Luke 17:6).

THE FOURTH COLLEGE

My fourth college in Penang was Systematic College. By this time, I already had fifteen years of lecturing experiences, and I was assigned to teach Paper 13 of the ACCA (UK). The boss of this college was a very nice man, Mr. Yeoh Ah Thor. I praise him greatly for his way of management, his ability to see the performance of each lecturer, and the way he rewarded each and every one according to his or her performance.

I thought I had no problems, but I was wrong. This was the first time when the accounting bodies were upgrading their papers, and I was much concerned with the accounting paper. I found that the syllabus and contents of the accounting paper kept changing as well. The moment I mastered certain topics of the accounting paper, the accounting bodies would announce changes to the contents. I felt very frustrated. I would not tell my students that I needed time to study the changes in the accounting paper. I had to teach the new contents immediately after the changes, and my students were waiting for my lecture of the new syllabus and new contents.

My head was swelling, and my heart was failing. I began to feel that I had to give up my profession forever. I cried for fear of losing my job as I had two children and a wife to feed. My family would have to face financial problems because I was the breadwinner of the family. I wept alone in my room as I felt so much emptiness and fear for I had no one to turn to. Then that long-forgotten voice whispered in my ears, and I recognized that voice, sweet and tender. That was the voice of Mother Mary, the mother of Jesus Christ.

She whispered in my ears, "When you are in trouble, let it be."

My fear and frustration then slowly melted away, and my thoughts turned positive. I let things be, and I went to sleep. Although I still did not understand all of the contents in the new syllabus, I woke up and felt a peace that I had never felt before. It was a Saturday morning, and I had no class to attend. I began reading the accounting textbook, but I still could not understand, and I knew I was still not ready to lecture on Monday. What to do? I took the book and read it aloud in the room just before I was about to sleep. Then I put the book under my head as a pillow and went to sleep soundly, for the peace of Mother Mary flowed in me.

When I woke up the next morning, I lectured to an imaginary class of students, for I had no work on Sunday. I felt that the ideas and understanding naturally flowed out from my mind. That Sunday night, I went to bed and slept soundly. The next morning was a

Monday, but I went to college happily, singing on my way to work. I entered my lecture room and lectured to a class of over thirty students taking the final financial accounting, Paper 13, of the Association of Certified and Chartered Accountants of UK (ACCA). It was a three-hour lecture, and I felt so satisfied and fulfilled as I had imparted my knowledge well.

Now, I had discovered a new method of studying. Before you go to sleep, you should call upon Jesus or Mother Mary to help you understand and remember what you read. Then you should open your book and read it quickly, going through as many pages as you can. Then put the book under your head as a pillow and go to sleep. Repeat the process every night until you finish the whole book.

Then you go for a second reading, using the same method above, finishing the whole book very quickly. This process should be repeated a third time. You will surely understand what you have read, for the mother of God had given the method I used to me, "Mother

Mary." Never have doubt in your mind, wondering if God will help you. Faith made Noah hear God's warnings about things in the future that he could not see. He obeyed God and built a boat in which he and his family were saved. As a result, the world was condemned, and Noah received the righteousness that comes by faith from God (Heb. 11:7).

A MAJOR TURN IN
MY CAREER

After lecturing at Systematic College for five years or so, I went to lecture at Stamford College, Penang. Here, I signed a contract with the directors of Stamford College. I would be paid a basic salary plus a 70 percent commission of the fees collected from the ICSA courses conducted in the evening. This ICSA Institute of Chartered Secretaries and Administrators (UK) program was a new course, and I started with zero students.

While the college paid for advertising and promotion, I had to build up the course myself. I could also choose the lecturers. Building up this course was my major concern, and I found the task heavy. My basic pay was low (RM 2500), so I had to rely heavily on the commission from the ICSA evening course to meet my expenses. I often prayed to Jesus to help me. All alone in the building, I prayed to Jesus in my own words. I used to say, "Jesus, You make the universe spin, and that force is great. With a spark of that force, You can turn my ICSA course to a success."

Did Jesus answer me? Yes! The number of ICSA students began to increase, and my commission increased as well. But because of the tremendous work pressure that I had to bear, my health began to deteriorate. I felt very tired and always wanting to sleep. I took many vitamin pills to get strong, but those didn't work.

A Price to Pay

I thought that the commission I earned would make me rich, but it did not because I was a great spender. I began to enjoy life and smoked heavily. As my commission climbed higher, I began to forsake my friend, Jesus. I thought I could go on happily without Him. For some time, I did go on happily without Jesus. I had forgotten what He had done for me.

I turned away from Him and followed Buddhist teachings. I went to Buddhist temples to pray. I thought that Buddhism would be richer and better, meaning it would make one to earn more money and help one to have better health. I went to take refuge with a Buddhist monk and chanted Buddhist sutras. I even followed the Buddhist way of honoring by saying "*Na Mo Oh Mi Toh Foh* (Honor to the Buddha who is coming in the future)."

I also went on a vegetarian diet to honor the Lord Buddha. I turned to the Lord Buddha for help. I asked Buddha for help to make me strong again. Did Buddha help me? I thought Buddha would not help a traitor like me. Anyway, something happened to turn me back to Jesus Christ. But all the time, when I turned away from Jesus, these words of Jesus to Peter kept ringing in my ears, "I tell you that before the rooster crows tonight, you will say three times that you do not know me." Peter then answered Jesus, "I will never say that even if I have to die with you" (Matt. 26:34–35). But as we all know, Peter did deny Jesus three times before the rooster crowed.

One day, a friend visited and asked me to take up an insurance policy. I still remember the name of the company, IHM. I had to go for a medical checkup before I could be insured, so I went to Penang Medical Centre (now called Gleneagles).

Upon the doctor's diagnosis, I was found to be suffering from blockage of my heart arteries. The doctor said I would die of heart failure if I didn't go for an operation soon. I was recommended to go for an open-heart bypass. My operation would cost RM 30,000, and I had no alternative but to undergo the operation soon, although I was poor. I had said earlier that I earned a lot, but I spent a lot, too.

I borrowed the RM 30,000 from my wife, and I went for the operation in 2000. My operation was done at Penang Adventist Hospital. When I was being pushed on my bed to the operation theater, I prayed to Jesus Christ to forgive me and help me to have a successful operation. The twelve-hour operation was a success.

After the operation, I became depressed and withdrew myself from people. I was afraid to meet people, and I thought of letting go and not caring for myself. I did not want to dress neatly. I dared not leave my house and only stayed at home for nearly ten years. When my daughter got married, I dared not attend her wedding dinner, and my daughter and my wife were very disappointed with me.

My wife took me to see a doctor, who told my wife that I had to seek the help of a psychiatrist. I refused to go to a psychiatrist, and I demanded to stay at home, claiming I was fine. In my mind, I knew I was not. It was so hard, and I felt impossible to pull myself out of that mental block. A doctor said I had to take an injection to cure me, but I would not submit to any cure.

To make matters worse, my friends said I was pretending to be mentally ill. They said I was a good actor and merely acting so I could avoid work. When relatives came to visit us, they would always tell others that I was merely acting so people would have pity on me. They all looked down on me and would tell others to avoid and ignore me. They did not understand mental depression and treated me as a madman who had no cure.

I refused to take normal meals, and I was afraid that I would die of hunger. I hated myself and everyone. I thought to myself, *Why on earth should I be born?* I never wanted anyone to buy food for me to eat, and I punished myself. Friends instigated others to go against me. Everyone said I was a good actor. I could even win an Academy Award for my "acting."

During this period of mental depression, I always asked, "Mother Mary, Jesus, and all the saints, why torment me?"

Nobody had the time to care for me, and with a little money left, I used to buy one loaf of bread to fill my stomach. I bought my bread from a man who would pass by my house on his motorcycle each day. I ordered my daily bread from this man, including Sundays. I did not have to step out from my house to buy bread.

During weekends, my wife would go out with her sister to eat out, and when they came back, they would buy a packet of noodles for me, and I felt so grateful. However, I dared not step out of my house to buy food for myself. I had lost hope in recovering. Although I was very unhappy, I dared not kill myself. I was baptized and confirmed at the church of Our Lady of Sorrows, and as a Catholic, suicide would be a great moral sin for God had created us and we belonged to God. Only God can take our life.

My life was not happy, and my friends ignored me. And for these ten years of mental depression, did Christ forget me, too? I remembered what Christ said when He was on the cross about to die—"Eli, Eli, lema sabachthani," which means "My God, My God, why did You abandon me?" (Matt. 27:46). I also began to say to myself, "My God, My God, why have You forsaken me?"

During this period of suffering, I used to hear a voice, calling me, "Foo, Ah Foo." And I would step down from my bed and look out from a window in my room. Each time I looked out, I could not find anybody.

Then I remembered what happened when Eve passed by the tree in the garden of Eden and a snake asked her, "Did God really tell you not to eat fruit from any tree in the garden?" The woman answered, "We may eat the fruit of any tree in the garden, except the tree in the middle of it. God told us not to eat the fruit of that tree or even touch it. If we do, we will die." The snake then replied, "That's not true. You will not die" (Gen. 3:1–4).

This voice that called me was like the snake in the garden of Eden. The voice wanted me to believe in that devil, but I told myself not to believe that voice. And if I did, I would be like Eve, who had fallen prey to the cunning devil. I waited for the Lord to pull me out of this deep ocean of depression. Many people do not know that depression is an illness, which is as equally serious as any critical physical illness. Externally, a depressed person may look well, but inwardly and mentally, he or she is sick. Depression can lead to insanity if not treated by a psychiatrist, and many people do not fully recover even after being treated by a psychiatrist.

But in my case, Jesus was behind me, and He was only testing me, although my trial was long. No psychiatrist had never treated me, yet I did not go insane. I only feared mingling with people so I would hide myself in my room whenever people came to visit us.

After much praying and pleading, Jesus finally came to help me, and He pulled me out of that deep ocean of depression. Jesus did not cure me instantly, like what He did to a paralyzed man who was lying on a bed (Matt. 9:6–7), but He cured me in a rather indirect way.

Jesus Had Mercy on Me

On September 9, 2010, my daughter gave birth to a boy. Later that night, a familiar voice whispered to me, telling me to go and see my grandson. I recognized that voice, so sweet and assuring, to be the voice of Mother Mary, the mother of Jesus. The next morning, I told my wife that I wanted to follow her to see my grandson. My wife and two children were surprised because I had not left my house in ten years. This was the first time I was leaving my house, and my purpose was to go and see my grandson. On my way to the confinement center, I felt so peaceful and so happy. I knew Jesus had lifted up my mental depression. Even without medication, I did not go insane. My case was like what Jesus did to a stormy sea.

Jesus got into a boat, and His disciples went with Him. Suddenly, a fierce storm hit the lake, and the boat was in danger of sinking, but Jesus was asleep. The disciples went to Him and woke Him up. "Save us, Lord," they said. "We are about to die." Jesus answered, "Why are you so frightened? What little faith you have?" Then He got up and ordered the winds and waves to stop, and there was a great calm (Matt. 8:23–26).

Yes, in my case, there was a great calm. Jesus had blessed me with a grandson to care for and to play with. He is now four years old and studying in kindergarten. I feel very happy taking care of him.

Never despair in times of difficulty, for God, who loves us so much that He gave His only Son to die for us so our sins could be forgiven and we could live in harmony with Him, doesn't like to see us suffer. Sometimes our sufferings are but temporary trials. Even Jesus was tested when He was a man like us. He was tested by the devil, who told Him to adore the devil so the devil would give Jesus the whole world. Have faith in Jesus, and He will surely help you like He had helped me many times. Jesus will help, although His help may come slowly.

MIGRAINE BOGGED ME DOWN

So far, so good, but I had been having a very serious impediment since very young. When I was in standard six, I suffered a very serious migraine attack. My mother had to wake in the middle of the night to get me some painkiller medicine. Sadly, we did not have any painkillers at home, not even Paracetamol, so my mother had to ask for two tablets from the neighbors. I swallowed the pills with some water. Then my mother massaged my head for about a half hour or so before my headache slowly melted away.

In time, these migraines would come more often, and the pain became increasingly severe with each attack. As I grew older, I searched everywhere for a cure. I took Chinese herbs, to no avail. I went to see doctor after doctor, but none could cure me.

Over the years, I was able to save some money, so I went to see a brain specialist at Penang Specialist Centre. He put me in a special machine that scanned my brain. After the scan, he told me that I had no brain tumor and I could relax. The specialist said I had migraines and gave me some Paracetamol plus some medicine called Carefergot for pain relief.

I prayed to Jesus to take away my headache, but He did not answer me. Every time I went outside on a hot day, I would suffer a migraine attack. The pain felt like needles piercing my brain! Each attack would send me crawling back to my bed or some dark place to close my eyes and relax. I had to lie down and not do anything.

On many occasions when I went fishing, I had to go home after a short while because my migraine would send me home to sleep. I could not enjoy an outdoor life. On several occasions, I took my son to a river to catch fish, but we could not stay there for long because my migraine headaches returned. Even the migraine would impede my studies.

I went to Christian groups for faith healing. They would place their hands on my head and call upon Jesus to help me, to take away my pain. They told me that I would see a bright light, but I saw nothing. I heard and felt nothing. *Perhaps my faith is not strong enough,* I thought. *Or, because I am a sinner, Jesus will not hear me.* A good friend of mine told me that I would finally go insane because of the never-ending torment. Yet all the while, I still clung on to Jesus. I had faith that He would answer my prayer one day, for Jesus said, "If you believe, you will receive whatever you ask for in prayer" (Matt. 21:22).

During this time of suffering, I did not turn away from Jesus to seek a cure from the devil. My friend told me that I could be cured if I submitted myself to

Satan. Although the temptation was great, I still clung to Jesus. I asked Him to at least enable me to study even though I had migraine attacks.

One day, Mother Mary whispered to me softly, "Patrick, let yourself go. Read and rest at intervals."

I did not understand what Mother Mary meant, so I tried to read my business law book. As I opened the book, I yawned. I felt very sleepy. Although I was half-asleep and half-awake, I still continued reading. I went on reading silently like this until I fell asleep. The next day, I read the book in that half-awake and half-asleep state until I could not stand it anymore and fell asleep. I went on reading like this until I finished the three-hundred-page book within a month. After that, I did a second reading in the same manner and read the book a third time using the same method.

Then I went to lecture business law to a tutorial class of working adults. My students thought I was a lawyer, but I told them I was not. I was able to lecture the whole business law subject in six months without having to bring any papers and notes to class. When I was assessed on the effectiveness of my lecturing, the students said they liked my class.

Mother Mary had helped me to discover a new method of studying!

The Sleep Method
of Studying

The above-mentioned method of studying is so effective and easy that I want to share it here. Mother Mary, the Mother of Perpetual Succor, the mother of Jesus Christ, gave me this gift. I call this the "sleep method of studying."

This study method works best when you are sleepy because, when your conscious mind is resting and dull, your subconscious mind would be active and receptive. Your subconscious mind can store information for a long time. In fact, information stored in the subconscious mind is never forgotten and is waiting for your decision to retrieve it. The longer the information is stored, the deeper it sinks into your subconscious, stored but never forgotten.

A path connects your conscious mind to your subconscious mind. When you tap your subconscious mind, it will send the stored information to your conscious mind. The longer the information is stored in your subconscious, the harder it will be for the subconscious mind to push the information you require to the conscious mind. The conscious mind then sees the information called for from the subconscious mind and allows you to express what you wish to convey. But the path leading from your conscious to the subconscious needs to be cleared (or polished) frequently for easier flow of information from the conscious to the subconscious mind and vice versa, just like a drain has to be cleared before the water can flow smoothly.

How are we going to polish the path that connects the conscious mind to subconscious mind? Yes, the path needs polishing before information can flow smoothly and quickly. The more we polish that path, the faster information flows from the subconscious to the conscious when the conscious mind calls for information. The process of polishing that path is via constant use and using it purposely and frequently.

Push information from the conscious mind to the subconscious mind, and let it digest in the subconscious mind. You may study something before bedtime and then go to sleep. Then, let what you have read sink into your subconscious mind, and let the digestion be done in your subconscious mind while you sleep. When your conscious mind is resting, your subconscious is working. The digested information is then pushed back from the subconscious to the conscious mind when you consciously recall the information the next morning when you awake.

Then try to understand what you had read the day before you went to sleep. Constantly and consistently polish that path this way. After some time, information stored becomes easier to be brought to the conscious mind. Then you will begin to understand that studying is not an obstacle anymore.

I tried this method many times. I tried it when I took the examinations of the Association of Business Executives (UK), the final fellowship examination of the Institute of Cost and Executive Accountants (UK), the advance diploma of the Chartered Institute of Marketing (UK), and my PhD in accounting and finance from Clayton University (USA). This method of studying helped me tremendously and never failed me, and I am sure that it will not fail you, too.

Never can this method fail because God had given it to me through the Blessed Virgin Mary, the mother of our Lord Jesus Christ. Yes, God is great. With the help of Jesus, I prepared for all my examinations (except my ABE diploma) by self-study at home, and I had not gone to any school or university.

The method can also be used to solve difficult problems, especially examination problems. I remember those days when I was lecturing the final financial accounting paper of the ACCA (UK). The examination questions set by this accounting body were very difficult and hard to solve. When I faced difficulty in solving these questions, I would use this method of study and at the same time pray to Jesus, "Jesus, You can make the universe spin as if a ball spins on an axis, and Your power is great. If You can give me a spark of Your power, I can solve all my problems, however difficult they may seem."

And miraculously, all my problems were solved. I could not leave any question unsolved because I had to face my class of students during my lecture. I had faith—and still do—that Jesus would help me in times of difficulties. Jesus had never failed me and will never fail me. Jesus will also not fail you. I repeat—Jesus had given me this method of study through the Blessed Virgin Mary, the mother of Jesus Christ. It will surely work if you follow the method sincerely and honestly.

Another miracle happened to me. My migraine headaches became increasingly lighter as I used this method of study. The frequency of migraine occurred less often, and the pain became progressively less severe. My daily life became increasingly fulfilling and satisfying. And at the age of sixty, my Lord Jesus Christ had fully cured my migraine. I have not suffered any migraine attack since then. I am now sixty-seven years old, and I lead a migraine-free life.

I am so happy!

MOTHER OF PERPETUAL SUCCOR HEARD ME

Yes, my migraine-free life led me to enjoy a happy life. Later, I began to supervise papers for various university examinations held at British Council, Penang. The examination subjects ranged from accounting and finance and management to business law. Students came from various colleges and institutions, and I had the help of tutors and lecturers. For me, I had to complete self-study at home for my examinations because I could not afford to go to university or college except when taking my ABE diploma. Unlike other students, I had no one to turn to for help to solve exam questions and understand the subject. But I had God. As I said earlier, God did help me with the gift of sleep method of studying, which I found—and still find—to be so effective. I am sure you will also gain from this secret, which the Lord Jesus had given to me through His mother, the Mother of Perpetual Succor.

The supervising went smoothly until I had a stomachache one day and had to go to the toilet. I passed black stools but did not know what it was. As I went back to the toilet a few more times and passed more black stool, I began to feel dizzy. I slowly began to pass what seemed to look like blood. The dizziness increased as I continued to pass more feces. I began to feel afraid, for I was fainting and felt like sleeping on the floor.

I asked my friend to take me home, and when I reached there, I asked my wife to take me to Penang General Hospital, a government-run hospital where I could be medicated and treated free of charge. Aided by my wife who took me by the arm, I went to the emergency department's admission counter. The clerk at the counter asked many questions, which I had no strength to answer. My wife gave all the answers and requirements on my behalf.

Finally, I was wheeled to the emergency ward so a doctor on duty could diagnose me. He suspected that I had some stomach problem, but because he did not know the exact cause of my bleeding, he wanted me admitted to the hospital. After recording my personal particulars and performing a further checkup, the hospital sent me to the ICU, where doctors and nurses would be available twenty-four hours a day. When I was in the ICU, the doctor on duty had to come to my bed to observe me. He found me passing bloodlike stool and collected them for examination. I had episode after episode of passing blood, and the doctors were quite concerned of whether I would survive or not.

One time when I was asleep, my legs protruded from the curtain that fenced my bed. The doctor saw my feet sticking out.

Thinking I was dead, he exclaimed, "Oh my God!"

But God was helping me, for the doctor's shout managed to wake me up. I slowly opened my eyes and looked at him.

"Aaah!" he sighed with relief.

I could not stand to pass motion; nor could I stand to pass urine. (Did he mean "stand up" or "*Tahan*"?) I was quite helpless, and nurses had to put a pan under my buttocks so I could do the needful. It was really inconvenient, as I had to wake up in the middle of the night for nurses to take my blood pressure, and they would prick my finger with a needle to get some blood to check my sugar level.

I was too obsessed with my own problems to care about what happened around me. All I knew was that many other patients were suffering the same fate as I had. All had stomach problems. Many had known their results and were waiting for the doctors' further action while patients were also waiting for the doctors' diagnoses.

I was waiting for the doctors to locate the site of my bleeding and the reason why I passed blood. I had to be given six pints of a blood transfusion before I could start to walk. I prayed to Jesus to help the doctors find the exact cause of my bleeding and the reason why I was passing blood in my motion. There were many patients in the hospital where the doctors could not find the exact cause of their illness. They had to wait much longer for the test and scan results before the doctors could take the necessary actions.

I prayed to Jesus to help me so I could be out of the ward quickly.

Then a voice spoke softly, "Patrick, be calm. You will be okay."

I recognized that sweet, soft voice. Yes, that was the voice of our Mother of Perpetual Succor, the mother of Jesus Christ.

The next morning, the nurses told me that I had to fast from midnight until the next day. The next day came, and I was pushed on my bed to a room for an endoscopy. The doctor inserted an endoscope into my mouth in order to take pictures of my intestine to see if there were any holes that caused me to pass blood in my motion. Yes, the doctor did find a hole the size a fifty-cent coin in my intestine. The process of inserting the endoscope from my mouth into the intestine was horrible. I wanted to vomit but could not bring out anything except some fluid, which flowed out from the side of my mouth. I wished the process would be over as soon as possible. But it seemed endless.

As they pushed the endoscope up and down my intestine to detect any hole there, I felt like I was going to die. I prayed for the process to end quickly but to no avail. The doctors thought there was more than one hole in my intestine. But to my relief, there was only one.

When the endoscopy finally ended, I was pushed on the wheelchair back to my bed in the same ward to await further action. They put me on twenty milligrams of Omeprazole. At first, I had to take one capsule before retiring at night, but after a follow-up session in the hospital, the doctor on duty increased the dosage to forty milligrams. I felt okay after that. Mother Mary, the Mother of Perpetual Succor, did indeed hear my prayer and granted me what I prayed for.

On many occasions, Jesus sent His mother to help me. Why send the mother, I do not know, but I do know what Christ had promised when one is faced with a problem.

"Ask and it will be given to you; seek and you will find; knock and the door will be opened to you. For everyone who asks receives; he who seeks finds and to Him who knocks, the door will be opened" (Matt. 7:7–8).

Have faith in Jesus in whatever difficult situation you are in. The Lord will certainly hear you. Even though He may be slow to respond, He will surely hear you and grant you what you asked for. He will surely come at an appropriate time. Never give up hope. Know that the good Lord may be testing you.

One Heart Artery Blocked Again

One day, I went to have some beer at a coffee shop. After drinking for a little while, I felt breathless. But once I stopped drinking, the symptom slowly subsided, and I felt okay. This symptom did not surface for a long time until I felt breathless one day when I climbed up a staircase. I was worried, and I kept this to myself. I also did not go to the hospital because I feared that the doctor would tell me something that I did not wish to hear. Then my feet swelled, and my fear became more intense. I told myself that the situation was okay and tried praying, but it did not work. I thought, *Perhaps I have asked too many favors from Him and He would not help me this time.*

I became restless and began thinking that perhaps my kidney, liver, or an internal organ was starting to fail. I even worried that I might have to go for kidney dialysis, a situation I feared most. I had heard that people with kidney failure had to go for dialysis every day until one dies. I was not afraid of death, but I was fearful of the suffering I would have to bear before the Lord finally took me away.

Day in and day out, I would worry until a voice whispered to me, saying, "Stop worrying. Go see a doctor."

I felt a sudden calm, and I recognized the voice, that sweet voice of our Mother Mary, the mother of Jesus Christ.

I went to Penang General Hospital (PGH) emergency ward for a checkup. After my open-heart surgery at Penang Adventist Hospital, I did not follow up with the doctors in Adventist because the charges were too expensive and I could not afford them. Instead, I made appointments to follow up with the doctors in PGH. As this was a government-run hospital, medication would be free for senior citizens. Even for ordinary Malaysians, the hospital charges would only be RM 5 per visit, and follow-up visits are practically free of charge.

I thank God that I can have free medication and free checkups. Without PGH, many people would have died because many patients cannot afford to go to private hospitals for treatment. The cost of care in private hospitals is increasing, and in this respect, we should learn to praise our government instead of criticize them all the time.

The doctor said I had to be warded because of my history of a heart bypass. The doctors wanted to have a more thorough examination before they could come to a conclusion.

During my stay in the cardiology ward of PGH, I realized the suffering of other human beings. All day long, I would hear patients groaning and crying, and I prayed for God to help ease their suffering. As I looked around, I found patients crawling on the floor and begging doctors to help them. The doctors on duty would rush to help patients, but they could not handle so many people at one time. Many patients had to bear great sufferings before the doctors could attend to them.

By looking at such suffering, I found my breathlessness to be a very minor complaint compared to the great sufferings that other patients had to bear. I told some patients to seek help from the Lord Jesus Christ, but they would not hear me. This was understandable as they were too obsessed by their own suffering to listen. Night after night and day after day, I prayed to the Lord to help the doctors to find out the cause of my breathlessness and my swollen legs.

After a few days in the ward, the doctors told me that they would put me on a coros procedure to find out how much of my artery was blocked. I was put on certain drugs before they could put me on test. I was told that the procedure was to insert a wire into my heart's artery via an opening in my hand or a soft spot between my thigh and body.

After much waiting, I was pushed in my bed to the operation theater. I could see many large lamps and bright lights, and many computers were in different places to enable the surgeons to see my arteries and heart. The doctors then made a small hole between my body and upper thigh before inserting a wire into the hole. From the computer, I was able to see my heart beating. I was very afraid. I could feel the wire being pushed close to my heart artery.

After a while, the doctors finished the procedure and pulled out the wire. Some attendants pushed my bed back to the ward, and I anxiously waited for the result.

The next morning, a lady doctor came to my bed and told me that my arteries were totally blocked. I was scared for my life. I was to get a letter of referral from her and then go to another hospital for a more detailed scan. I went to see a doctor in the other hospital about a month later. The scan revealed one artery to be completely blocked. The hospital then sent a detailed report plus an x-ray back to the doctor at PGH.

After several months of waiting, I went for my follow-up appointment at the heart specialist clinic of PGH. The doctor told me that they would insert a stent into my blocked artery. The doctor then asked the nurse to arrange an appointment. My stent was to be done in three months. But I wanted to end my suffering as soon as possible. The wait seemed like a very long period of time.

I became nervous and started to worry. My mind turned negative, and I felt the worst would happen. But I pressed ahead with prayer, and a voice told me to relax. Then I remembered the words to the song "Let It Be" by the Beatles, "When I was in trouble, Mother Mary speaks to me, whispering words of wisdom, let it be, let it be, let it be." As I began to sing that song, I began to feel more at ease and relaxed. I was able to do my daily chores. I stopped worrying and started living again.

During the three months of waiting, I realized that I could relax after listening to soothing songs, especially church hymns. Sunday mass in church became a time of relaxation while praising God rather than just a day of mere obligation. I loved to go to church. Now I loved going to church even more since I found solace in the Lord. It is not enough that we praise the Lord, but we must feel that we are in union with Him and that He takes charge of our lives. He will hold our hand and guide us, and He will help us conquer all mountains and obstacles in our journey in life until we meet the Lord in His Father's house. Christ said that, in His Father's house, there are many rooms and He will prepare a place for us (John 14:2). But meanwhile on earth, He will see us through. Wait for the Lord, and He will surely come to you when you are in trouble. Jesus had said, "Carry my yoke and it would be light"

(Matt. 11:30). Yes, carry the burdens of life, and He will lighten them.

Finally, the big day came. I was admitted to the cardiology ward one day before the operation. The nurse monitored my blood pressure and blood sugar level. The patient in the bed beside mine could not go for the stent operation because his sugar level and blood pressure was too high. He would have to wait until all readings became normal before he could be operated on. I prayed that my readings would be normal so I could go for the stent operation without delay. I had been waiting for this day for a long time, and I did not wish to wait anymore.

The next day at about noon, the hospital attendants came and brought me some clothes to wear during the operation before pushing my bed to the operating theater. On my way to the theater, I prayed, "Jesus, have mercy on me. Jesus, heal me. Jesus, save me. Jesus, free me."

I repeated this prayer repeatedly until I finally reached the operating room. I waited a long time for my turn. I was not given any anesthetic, so I was aware of what was going on around me. The surgeon made a small opening in the area between my upper thigh and body, and then he inserted a thin wire into the small opening. A doctor using a computer gave instructions to the operating surgeon to move the wire to an area in an artery where he could place the stent. I could see and hear everything going on. It was fearful indeed. All this while, I prayed to Jesus to help me. I prayed that the operation would be a success.

But the operation did not turn out well. I heard the operating surgeon exclaim in a loud and steady voice that he wanted a longer wire. The nurse went to search for a longer wire, but she came back saying that she could not find such a wire.

The doctor then pulled out the wire, which was in my heart artery, and postponed the whole operation. My heart sank. Why Jesus didn't help me, I did not know. I was then pushed back on a bed to my ward, and the nurse prepared my summary discharge. I did not understand the contents of the discharge. She gave me a new appointment date, three months later. Meanwhile, the doctor prescribed an additional drug called frusemide (forty milligrams). I took my other medicines plus this new one, and the swelling of my legs subsided.

Yes, with Jesus's help, the doctors had given me the right medication. My breathlessness also became lighter. Although the operation was not a success, at least the medication helped to bring down the swelling of my legs and lessen my breathlessness. Without the help of Jesus, all these good things would not come. All good things come from Him. Hallelujah!

As I was waiting for the three months to pass, I used to go to a small chapel with a statue of Mother Mary. I asked Mother Mary to implore her son, Jesus, to help me on the day of the operation. I prayed that Jesus would guide the doctors in the operation and make it a success. I also said to Jesus, "Open the eyes of the doctors so they can see and take a correct course of action."

When I was about to go to bed one night, Mother Mary softly spoke to me, "Your prayer will be heard."

Finally, the day before the stent operation arrived. Again, I was admitted to the cardiology ward one day before the operation. Again, I prayed to Jesus, and I said, "Jesus, open the eyes of the doctors so they can see and take the correct course of action."

The next day, the attendants came and asked me to put on the clothes for the operation. I felt nervous and hoped that the doctors would do a good job. After putting on the clothes, I slept on my bed, and the attendants pushed my bed to the operating room. Then my turn arrived, but the doctors told me that they had lost my file. I was scared out of my life. The doctors then phoned the administration department for my file, but they could not find it.

Again, my operation had to be postponed. I asked myself why the doctors were unable to perform the operation on me. Then, I turned to Jesus and asked, "Why, Jesus? Why?"

In the ward, I waited for the nurse to give me a new date for the stent operation. Again, I had to wait for another three months.

As I waited for the three months to come, I continued to talk to Mother Mary. I asked her why the stent operation could not be done. I asked her if she had something better in store for me. I took the doctor's discharge summary, placed it in front of the statue of Mother Mary, and asked her to give guidance and help the doctors to take a correct course of action. I was thinking in my mind, *Why, Mother Mary, did you say these words to me previously: Your prayer will be heard.* Then, I wondered, *When would Christ hear me?*

Once again, the day of the stent operation finally arrived. I was admitted to the cardiology ward one day before the operation as usual. While in the ward, I prayed to Jesus again, asking Him to help the doctors perform a successful operation. At night, I began to have bad dreams. I dreamed of my deceased mother calling me to join her. I dreamed of entering into hell, and all sorts of ghosts were appearing before me in hell. I called out loudly for help, and I finally awoke to find myself lying on my bed. After a while, two attendants came to my bedside and asked me to put on the clothes for the operation.

After I had put on the clothes, I was pushed on my bed to the operating theater. I waited for some time in the operating room before my turn came for the operation. As usual, the doctors made a small opening in the space between my upper thigh and body. The surgeon then inserted a wire through that opening and pushed the wire into my heart artery. After some time, the surgeon announced that my artery was totally blocked and the stent could not be inserted into the artery. Then the surgeon pulled out the wire and said that the stent operation could not be done. He told me that my other arteries were still functioning well and there was no danger of a heart failure. The attendants then pushed my bed with me in it, back to the cardiology ward.

The next morning, a doctor came and told me that nothing else could be done. The doctor said that they would monitor my condition and would perform a second open-heart bypass when it would be necessary to do so. Now I began to understand what Mother Mary meant when she said, "Your prayer will be heard." Mother Mary used the future tense "will" to mean "next time."

The current situation did not need any help, but when the second open-heart bypass came, then Jesus would help me. Jesus had not failed me before, and He would not fail me in the future, meaning the second open-heart bypass. Mother Mary always came to visit me at an appropriate time.

Hail, Mother Mary, full of grace! Hallelujah! Hallelujah!

Mother Mary Whispered to Me

I thought everything would be well after the doctor had cured me of my first stomach ulcer attack. I ate everything as usual, and I did not feel any pain in my stomach. I took sour foods like laksa and fish curry, taboo foods that stomach ulcer patients should not take. I believed I was fully cured and no food was taboo to me. I enjoyed many delicious meals, not knowing that these foods were slowly causing my stomach ulcer to relapse. I was looking for trouble because of my own ignorance. I could not blame anybody.

One day, I felt my stomach bloated. Thinking it was just some food I ate, I took some medicine, and the bloating subsided. I returned to my work without any thought of the bloated stomach. Later, I began to pass some liquid stool. Then the stool became increasingly darker, and I began to feel faint. My wife quickly took me to PGH. There, the doctor looked at my eyes and realized they were pale. Indeed, my eyelids were pale, and I had to be warded.

In the ward, I began to pass blood and had to be given six pints of blood. I slowly became increasingly stronger. The doctors gave me some medicines. I did not ask what they were for. All I knew was my feces turned yellow in color after taking those medicines. While all this hullabaloo was going on, I forgot to pray. I was thinking that all would turn out well as it did when I first passed blood from my anus. Jesus faded from my mind as I felt myself becoming progressively stronger each day while I was staying in the ward.

After several days of observation and care, a nurse told me that I had to go for an endoscopy. The next morning, two attendants came to my bedside and pushed my bed to the endoscopy room. In the room, a doctor sprayed some anesthetic into my throat and then slowly and steadily pushed an endoscope through my mouth into my stomach. The process took about a half hour as the doctor pushed the endoscope down and pulled it up in my intestine. I felt so terrible, and I felt like dying. From the side of my mouth, I vomited out a lot of fluid onto the bed.

But after suffering this endoscopy, the doctor could find no ulcer and did not know the cause of the passing of blood. I became very afraid, fearful that the cause would be something that I dreaded most, cancer. If it were cancer, I thought it would be the end. Out of desperation, the name of Jesus rushed into my thick head. I softly called out to Jesus to help me, to help the doctors to find out the real cause of my passing of blood.

That night in the ward, I could not sleep. I tossed about in my bed, and I would sit up and pray to God. I implored God to hear me and to grant my wish. I wanted to know the cause of the passing of blood from my anus.

The next morning, a nurse told me that I had to undergo another endoscopy, but this time, it would be through the anus. I thought that this process would be better than the endoscopy through my mouth.

Later that afternoon, two attendants came to my bedside and pushed the bed to the endoscopy room. The doctor injected some anesthetic to make me feel numb. Once the anesthetic took effect, an endoscope was pushed into my anus to reach my intestine. I felt painful, and I told the doctor, "Pain! Pain!"

The doctor gave me another injection, but I still felt pain. The doctor then asked me to bear the pain a little while longer. He then pushed the endoscope from my anus to the colon. The process was very slow as the endoscope passed through my intestine to reach my colon.

The process was very painful to me, and in my pain, I prayed to Jesus to help me, to reduce my pain, and to help me have the power to endure my pain until the end. I prayed, and the doctor finally announced that he had reached the colon. I sighed silently and thanked Jesus.

The most anxious moment was the wait for the doctor's findings. I waited for the diagnosis and hoped that the doctor would say that an ulcer was found in my intestine. To my surprise, the doctor told me that my intestine and colon was clear and there was no ulcer. Then I thought to myself, *Cancer must have caused the passing of blood from my anus!* I was very worried for I did not know the cause of the bleeding. When I was in the ward, I couldn't sleep, and I was restless.

I began to pray to Mother Mary, "Please understand my suffering and shed light on my darkness over the cause of my bleeding. You surely understand me, for you had also suffered more than this when you saw Jesus, your son, being crucified on the cross."

Having said this prayer, I felt a calm, and I heard a soft voice whisper, "Your prayer is heard. Go to sleep, and peace be with you."

That night, I slept soundly, and I did not worry at all.

The next morning, a nurse stood at my bedside and told me that I had to go for a second endoscopy. In the afternoon, two attendants arrived to push my bed to the endoscopy room. This time, the endoscope was put into my mouth to reach my intestine. The process was very painful, and I felt utter suffering, yet I was able to bear this pain for I was confident that the cause of my bleeding would be found.

I knew and had faith that Jesus would help me, for He had sent His mother to me last night. After about a half hour, the process was over, and again, I waited anxiously for the doctor's diagnosis. Finally, the doctor told me that I had several peptic ulcers in my stomach. I sighed with relief. Finally, all had ended well. I thanked Jesus for guiding the doctor to find my cause of bleeding. It was indeed a miracle that the doctor could find the cause of my bleeding during the second endoscopy when he could not find the cause of bleeding after the first.

God is great! God is great! Hallelujah! Hallelujah!

Indeed, God is great! I had started praying to Jesus in my childhood. He had never failed me. Have faith in Jesus in whatever difficult circumstances you are in, and surely He will listen to your prayer. Believe, and He will surely come to your aid. On some occasions, Jesus may not come to help you personally, but He will surely send one of His helpers: Mother Mary, Saint Anne, Saint Peter, or even an angel or one of His disciples. Never give up hope, for, as far as I am concerned, Jesus has never failed me, and He never fails us. Many do not get the help of Jesus because they lack faith. For Jesus said, "If you have faith as small as a mustard seed, you can say to this mountain, 'Move from here to there,' and it will move. Nothing will be impossible for you" (Matt. 17:20).

Yes, nothing shall be impossible. Only believe and have faith. The words of Jesus can never come to nothing. God is compassionate. God is love. God is forgiving. God is always there. Just ask, and it shall be given. If Jesus could raise the dead, your and my problems are nothing compared to the raising of the dead. Amen!

Let us join hands to praise Jesus. The more people pray together, the more powerful is our prayer. I conclude here by quoting the lyrics of a church hymn often sung at masses in church services.

What a Friend We Have in Jesus

1

What a friend we have in Jesus,

All our sins and griefs to bear;

What a privilege to carry;

Everything to God in prayer.

Oh, what peace we often forfeit,

Oh, what needless pain we bear;

All because we do not carry;

Everything to God in prayer.

2

Have we trials and temptations?
Is there trouble anywhere?
We should never be discouraged,
Take it to the Lord in prayer.

Can we find a friend so faithful,
Who will all our sorrows share?
Jesus knows our every weakness,
Take it to the Lord in prayer.

3

Are we weak and heavy laden,
Cumbered with a load of care?
Precious Saviour still our refuge,
Take it to the Lord in prayer.

Do thy friends despise, forsake thee?

Take it to the Lord in prayer.

In His arms He'll take and shield thee,

Thou wilt find a solace there.